# TWIN FALLS SAUCER HOAX SIMPLIFIED

# TWIN FALLS SAUCER HOAX SIMPLIFIED

SOLOMON HATHAWAY

Revitalized Occult and Strange

Published by Revitalized Occult and Strange, an imprint of Bald and Bonkers Network LLC.

ISBN/SKU: 979-8-3302-6600-5
EISBN: 979-8-3302-6601-2

This is a work of non-fiction. While every effort has been made to ensure the accuracy of the information contained herein, the publisher and author assume no responsibility for errors or omissions, or for damages that may result from the use of the information contained in this book.
Artificial intelligence was used in the editorial process to assist in grammar correction, content organization, and ensuring clarity and coherence of the text.

# CONTENTS

# CHAPTER 1

# Introduction Summary

The Twin Falls saucer hoax involved a fabricated flying disc found in Twin Falls, Idaho, on July 11, 1947. During a period of widespread reported sightings of "flying discs" across the nation, Twin Falls citizens claimed to have retrieved a "disc" measuring 30 inches (76 cm). The FBI and Army authorities seized the disc and promptly declared it a hoax. The media disclosed that local teenagers had confessed to orchestrating the hoax. Additionally, it is noteworthy that Idaho has been identified as a probable hotspot for UFO activity in the 2020s.

# CHAPTER 2

# History Leading up to the Hoax

On June 24, 1947, civilian pilot Kenneth Arnold reported seeing 'flying discs,' a sighting that sparked nationwide reports by June 27.

The Twin Falls Times-News announced on July 1 that "flying saucers have invaded" the Twin Falls area following a report by a forest ranger and his companion. They claimed to have observed eight to ten "discs" in a V-formation over Galena Summit. While marking timber three miles south of the summit, they heard a buzzing sound and spotted the shining objects overhead. Walter Nicholson, one of the witnesses, stated that the objects bore no resemblance to any known aircraft.

On July 2, a second UFO sighting was reported by the press. Mr. and Mrs. J. F. Meuser, while driving near Malta, Idaho, observed what they described as a solitary, luminous object resembling a "big ball of fire," comparable in size to the moon but significantly brighter.

The next day, on July 3, a third sighting occurred. B.G. Tiffany, a railway foreman, recounted to the Times-News that he and his crew had witnessed a formation of nine disc-shaped objects flying silently in a V-formation over Hollister, Idaho, an event that had taken place a month earlier. On July 4, additional reports emerged. R.L. Dempsey, a resident of Twin Falls, claimed to have seen two such discs above the city, and in Richfield, Idaho, three individuals reported observing a single disc.

On July 5, a gathering of 60 individuals engaging in a picnic in Twin Falls observed 35 disc-shaped objects in the sky, which was reported by the local press as the "most significant number of these mysterious devices seen anywhere in the nation." Two days later, on July 7, there were additional reports of sightings, including one involving three teenagers who described seeing a solitary disc approximately the size of a motor scooter wheel.

This event in Twin Falls was not an isolated incident. On July 8, reports emerged that Army personnel at Roswell had retrieved a 'flying disc.' However, this claim was quickly retracted, and the following day, the debris was identified as a common weather balloon. The flurry of sightings culminated on July 10 with a report from United Press about a purported hoax saucer found in North Hollywood.

# CHAPTER 3

# UFO "Crash" in Twin Falls

On July 11, media outlets reported the retrieval of a 30-inch disc from a residence in Twin Falls. The locals had heard a significant noise at approximately 2:30 am, which they initially thought was a truck. However, by 8:20 am, a neighbor found the disc and alerted the authorities. The local police secured the item and escalated the situation to the FBI and military intelligence. Officers from Fort Douglas were dispatched to conduct a thorough investigation. The authorities maintained secrecy over the incident until further details could be ascertained. The press covered the military's secretive approach to the investigation, noting that photographs of the disc were seized. Subsequently, the FBI announced that the disc had been handed over to the Army. The following day, it was revealed that the disc was a fabricated hoax by four teenagers, and photographs of the disc were released to the public.

## Description

The described object contained radio tubes, electric coils, and wires beneath a plexiglass dome. Deseret News reported that the disc was thirty inches across, akin to the base of an antiquated chandelier, featuring a plexiglass bubble on one side and a steel counterpart on the other. Within the plastic dome, three silver-painted radio tubes were connected to what seemed to be an electromagnetic coil on the exterior. The Independent Record added that the object had a diameter of 30.5 inches, with a metallic dome on one side and a 14-inch high plastic dome on the other, secured by what looked like stove bolts. The device was gold-painted on one side and silver on the other, suggesting it was machine-produced.

### *Reception and influence*

The Twin Falls incident, which gained national attention through a widely circulated photograph of a nonplussed army officer holding a disc-shaped object of simple design, has been dubbed the final blow to the media frenzy surrounding the 1947 flying disc phenomenon. Following this event, there was a notable decline in press coverage.

The Twin Falls event, however, was not the concluding episode in the series of saucer recovery hoaxes. Merely weeks later, on July 28, 1947, there emerged claims of disc debris retrieval at Maury Island, Washington. Subsequently, in 1949, the narrative of a downed disc became part of the Aztec, New Mexico UFO hoax. In later years, peripheral conspiracy theorists such as Kenn Thomas and Nick Redfern would invoke the Twin Falls hoax, linking it to broader UFO conspiracy theories and even the assassination of President John F. Kennedy.

# 8  –   SOLOMON HATHAWAY

## REFERENCES

1. "Speedy 'Flying Saucers' Now Being Reported Throughout United States." *The Times-News*, Twin Falls, Idaho, June 27, 1947, p. 1.

2. "'Flying Discs' Reported Soaring Over Galena in Wavering 'V' Formation." *The Times-News*, Twin Falls, Idaho, July 1, 1947, p. 1.

3. "Solo Disc Reported at Malta." *The Times-News*, Twin Falls, Idaho, July 2, 1947, p. 1.

4. "More Discs Reports as U.S. Opens Probe." *The Times-News*, Twin Falls, Idaho, July 3, 1947, p. 1.

5. "'Flying Discs' Seen Over City, Richfield." *The Times-News*, Twin Falls, Idaho, July 4, 1947, p. 1.

6. "'Flying Saucers' Seen by 16 More Residents of Area." *The Times-News*, Twin Falls, Idaho, July 7, 1947, p. 1.

7. "'Weather Balloon,' Says AAF of New Mexico's 'Saucer'." *The Times-News*, Twin Falls, Idaho, July 9, 1947, p. 1.

8. "'Jokers' Have Great Fun on 'Flying Discs'." *The Times-News*, Twin Falls, Idaho, July 10, 1947, p. 1.

9. Jacobson, David J. "The Affairs of Dame Rumor." Rinehart, November 24, 1948 – via Google Books.

10. Bloecher, Ted. "Report on the UFO Wave of 1947." November 24, 1967 – via Google Books.

11. Weeks, Andy. *Forgotten Tales of Idaho.* Arcadia Publishing, March 30, 2015. ISBN 9781625852465 – via Google Books.

12. "'Disc' Found In Yard Here Causes 'Stir'." *The Times-News*, Twin Falls, Idaho, July 11, 1947, p. 2.

13. Randle, Kevin D. *Crash: When UFOs Fall From the Sky: A History of Famous Incidents, Conspiracies, and Cover-Ups.* Red Wheel/Weiser, May 20, 2010. ISBN 9781601637369 – via Google Books.

14. "4 'Ambitious' Youths Given 'Disc' Credit." *The Times-News*, Twin Falls, Idaho, July 13, 1947, p. 2.

15. "Attention Focuses On City as 'Disc' Is Found in Yard." *The Times-News*, Twin Falls, Idaho, July 11, 1947, p. 1.

16. "The 'Disc' Investigation." *The Times-News*, Twin Falls, Idaho, July 15, 1947, p. 4.

17. "Flying Disc Reported Found in Idaho; Now in Army Hands." *The Independent-Record*, July 11, 1947, p. 1.

18. "Twin Falls Falling Disc Proves Ingenious Hoax Of 4 Teen-age Boys." *Deseret News*, July 12, 1947, p. 9.

19. Wright, Susan. *UFO Headquarters: Investigations On Current Extraterrestrial Activity In Area 51.* St. Martin's Publishing Group, August 15, 1998. ISBN 9780312207816 – via Google Books.

20. "Army Will Explain Crash of Plane Carrying Saucer." *The Neosho Daily News*, Neosho, Missouri, August 5, 1947, p. 4. Retrieved November 29, 2022.

21. Shaw, Herbert A. "New Book Revives Flying Saucer Controversy: Attacks A.F. Role." *Dayton Daily News*, Dayton, Ohio, September 8, 1950, p. 31. Retrieved November 29, 2022.

22. "Aliens planned John F. Kennedy's

assassination, claims author." *Business Standard India*, March 23, 2015 – via Business Standard.

23. "FBI's real-life 'X-Files' documents strange connection between UFOs and the JFK assassination." *MuckRock*.

24. Russell, Stefene. "Stalking the Octopus." *stlmag.com*, July 24, 2008.

www.ingramcontent.com/pod-product-compliance
Lightning Source LLC
Chambersburg PA
CBHW051337160726
47995CB00004B/1122
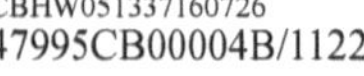